Facts About the Flamingo

By Lisa Strattin

© 2019 Lisa Strattin

Revised 2022 © Lisa Strattin

FREE BOOK

FREE FOR ALL SUBSCRIBERS

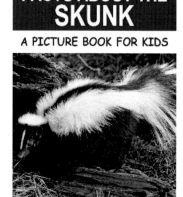

LisaStrattin.com/Subscribe-Here

BOX SET

- **FACTS ABOUT THE POISON DART FROGS**
- **FACTS ABOUT THE THREE TOED SLOTH**
  - **FACTS ABOUT THE RED PANDA**
  - **FACTS ABOUT THE SEAHORSE**
  - **FACTS ABOUT THE PLATYPUS**
  - **FACTS ABOUT THE REINDEER**
  - **FACTS ABOUT THE PANTHER**
- **FACTS ABOUT THE SIBERIAN HUSKY**

LisaStrattin.com/BookBundle

Facts for Kids Picture Books by Lisa Strattin

Little Blue Penguin, Vol 92

Chipmunk, Vol 5

Frilled Lizard, Vol 39

Blue and Gold Macaw, Vol 13

Poison Dart Frogs, Vol 50

Blue Tarantula, Vol 115

African Elephants, Vol 8

Amur Leopard, Vol 89

Sabre Tooth Tiger, Vol 167

Baboon, Vol 174

Sign Up for New Release Emails Here

LisaStrattin.com/subscribe-here

COVER IMAGE

****ADDITIONAL IMAGES****

Contents

INTRODUCTION

The flamingo is a large colorful bird found both in South America and Africa. The flamingo is also found in the warmer areas of southern Europe and western Asia.

There are six different species of flamingo found around the world. The Greater Flamingo which is the most widespread species of flamingo found in Africa, Southern Europe, and Southern Asia. The Lesser Flamingo is the most numerous species and is found in Africa and Northern India. The Chilean Flamingo is a large species that is found in South America. The James's Flamingo is a small and delicate species found in the Andes mountains in Peru, Chile, Bolivia, and Argentina. The Andean Flamingo is closely related to the James's Flamingo and is also found in the Andes mountains in Peru, Chile, Bolivia, and Argentina. The American Flamingo is a large species found in the Caribbean and the Galapagos islands.

CHARACTERISTICS

The flamingo stays in flocks of up to around 200 birds and feeds on fish in quiet-running rivers and lakes.

The flamingo is often seen on the banks of the lake standing on one leg. It is actually sleeping when it is on one leg, but the strange thing is, that only half of the flamingo is actually asleep - the half that controls the leg still standing remains active! The flamingo then swaps over so that the remaining side can get some rest and the side that was sleeping becomes active again.

APPEARANCE

Most species of flamingo are a pinky/orange color, some however can be white, black, or even blue. The color of the flamingo comes from the flamingo's diet, this is what turns the flamingo into the bright pink bird that we are so accustomed to seeing.

LIFE STAGES

Although flamingos only nest once a year, their colonies are known to breed at any time of the year. A flamingo reaches sexual maturity (which means the bird is able to breed) when it is between 3 and 6 years old.

Flamingos build their nests out of mud, stones and feathers and do this about 6 weeks before they lay their eggs. They tend to lay just one egg that hatches after a 30-day incubation period. Both the mother and the father are known to help to raise the chick.

LIFE SPAN

The flamingo usually grows to be about 30 years old although it is not uncommon for some flamingos to be as old as 50 years!

SIZE

The adult flamingo is usually over 3 feet tall and can be almost 5 feet tall! The wingspan is longer than its height, generally from 5 to 6 feet from wingtip to wingtip and they can weigh as much as 4 to 9 pounds.

HABITAT

The flamingos are termed a waterfowl, so they live near water. Preferred are large lakes and lagoons. They stand in the shallow water and pull food out of the water with their beaks.

DIET

The flamingo uses it's strangely shaped upside-down beak to separate mud and food in the water, filtering shrimp from it that they like to eat. The mouth of the flamingo is covered in little hairs called lamellae and a rough tongue which both help in this filtering activity.

ENEMIES

Flamingos have relatively few predators in the wild, but this is dependent on where it lives. Wild dogs and crocodiles are the main threats of the flamingo, along with eagles that prey upon the flamingo eggs and vulnerable chicks.

SUITABILITY AS PETS

It would be difficult to have a flamingo as a pet. They need to be able to filter food from the water where they live, so you would have to keep any lagoon stocked with the appropriate food for them. They also don't really like it when humans come close to them and will usually run away. It is best to visit a zoo or a preserve, or even an area where they live in the wild, if you want to watch them.

COLOR ME

COLOR ME

COLOR ME

COLOR ME

COLOR ME

COLOR ME

COLOR ME

COLOR ME

COLOR ME

COLOR ME

Please leave me a review here:

LisaStrattin.com/Review-Vol-195

For more Kindle Downloads Visit Lisa Strattin Author Page on Amazon Author Central

amazon.com/author/lisastrattin

To see upcoming titles, visit my website at LisaStrattin.com– most books available on Kindle!

LisaStrattin.com

FREE BOOK

FOR ALL SUBSCRIBERS – SIGN UP NOW

LisaStrattin.com/Subscribe-Here

LisaStrattin.com/Facebook

LisaStrattin.com/Youtube

Made in United States
North Haven, CT
20 March 2024